Vocabulary Rhyminders

Brett Peterson

Rhyminders © 2010

<u>Vocabulary Rhyminders</u>

About Rhyminders

I first started creating vocabulary rhymes as preparation for college entrance exams. This fun mnemonic device allowed me to achieve a perfect score on the reading portion of the ACT. Later I used the same technique to achieve an excellent score on the verbal section of the GRE and attend George Washington University for graduate school.

I designed Rhyminders to be a fun and innovative learning experience. The book is packed with memorable rhymes to help people of all ages learn and remember difficult words and concepts.

If you have any questions, suggestions, or comments, please feel free to email me or join me on the Rhyminders page on Facebook.

Have fun rhyming and best of luck!

Brett

brett@rhyminders.com

How To Use This Book

Rhyminders turns the mundane process of learning difficult vocabulary words into a fun and enjoyable experience. Every rhyme is created to be as easy to memorize as possible and designed to create a mental image that will stick with you until test day and beyond. Always say the rhymes out loud! This is the best way to learn and remember the difficult vocabulary words included in this book.

Sample (part of speech) definition

This is a **sample**
Vocabulary rhyme
Make sure to say it
Out loud every time

A special thanks to Norton Juster for teaching me about Rhyme and Reason.

And to Liz and Natalie for their editing expertise.

Abase (v) to degrade

To add insult to injury
The man was **abased**
Handcuffed, insulted and
Degradingly maced

Abate (v) to lessen

Planned a picnic today
The rain won't **abate**
It just won't end
Must be our fate

Abdicate (v) to resign

The king is forced to leave
And **abdicate** his throne
The country in upheaval
Its future is unknown

Abduct (v) to kidnap

The school mascot was missing
Abducted one dark night
Our rival school was suspected
Of keeping him from sight

Aberration (n) deviation

No peanut butter for lunch?
That's an **aberration** for real
It seems I have PB&J
Almost every single meal

Abet (v) to assist

The crook has a plan
The banker aids and **abets**
Got caught stealing millions
They now have many regrets

Abhor (v) to despise

Pacifist by nature
Violence he **abhors**
Looking for solutions
To prevent future wars

Abide (v) to accept

Sara was grounded for 2 weeks
She had no choice but to **abide**
Not wanting to take the chance
Of getting on her Dad's bad side

Abject (adj) miserable

A sure way to live
In **abject** poverty
Is to spend every day
Playing the state lottery

Abjure (v) to abandon

Class President Steve
Abjured his position
He left the post
On his own volition

Abridge (v) to shorten

That book is way too thick
Is there an **abridged** version?
It is sad to say but
I have a big book aversion

Abscond (v) to leave secretly

Thinking no one was looking
Sam **absconded** with the candy
But he was quickly spotted
By the lunch lady Sandy

Abstain (v) to go without

Peer pressure is difficult
But sometimes you must **abstain**
From the decisions friends make
Which go against your grain

Acclaim (n) praise

Desperately wanting
Attention and **acclaim**
The actor worked hard
For fortune and fame

Accolades (n) awards

Kim was a fantastic singer
Right from the start
She picked up **accolades**
While topping the charts

Accord (n) agreement

After the grueling war
They signed an **accord**
Which gave many hope
Peace would be restored

<u>Accost</u> (v) to confront

The mean bully
Accosted the boy
He yelled, screamed
And took his toy

<u>Acerbic</u> (adj) sour

That lemon is **acerbic**
Bitter and sour
Not a food you're
Likely to devour

<u>Acrimony</u> (n) bitterness

After a bad breakup
Acrimony will appear
Accusations and insults
You're certain to hear

<u>Acumen</u> (n) intellect

Bob's strong work ethic
And math **acumen**
Will keep him from
A life of vacuumin'

Acute (adj) severe

The doctor said the pain was **acute**
It was sharp and severe
Cute was the last thing
Fred expected to hear

Adamant (adj) firm

The school was very harsh
Adamant about being on time
Being late to class
Was treated like a crime

Adhere (v) to follow

We trusted our leader
And **adhered** to the plan
Loyal to the cause
The journey began

Admonish (v) to criticize

My mom didn't like it
And **admonished** me the most
For our ill fated plan
Of hitchhiking to the coast

<u>Adulation</u> (n) praise

After earning his diploma
Jon received **adulation**
Pats on the back
And congratulation

<u>Adverse</u> (adj) unfavorable

The wicked weather
Was much too **adverse**
If we ski today
We could end up in a hearse

<u>Advocate</u> (v) to support

The group **advocated**
They actively promoted
A cause for which
They were dearly devoted

<u>Aesthetically</u> (adv) artistically

The room's interior design
Is **aesthetically** pleasing
The fireplace is stylish
And could keep us from freezing

Affable (adj) friendly

Sarah was **affable**
Friendly and nice
Had many friends
Gave good advice

Affinity (n) attraction

A person with a great **affinity**
For planets and stars
Knows the difference between
Saturn and Mars

Affluent (adj) wealthy

The ball player was **affluent**
He was wealthy and rich
He earned his money
From his fastball pitch

Affront (n) insult

Tim was insulted
He took it as an **affront**
That someone in line
Would cut in front

Agnostic (adj) nonbeliever

When he couldn't find evidence
That was diagnostic
Rob gave up religion
And became **agnostic**

Aisle (n) passageway

In the church
You stand in file
As you walk
Down the **aisle**

Allay (v) to relieve

I comforted her and
Allayed her fears
By stopping the pain
And holding her dear

Alleviate (v) to ease

The elderly man said
The drug **alleviates** the pain
Making it possible to
Walk without a cane

Allocate (v) to assign

The school funds
Were not evenly split
But **allocated**
How the teacher saw fit

Altercation (n) argument

An **altercation** is a fight
Usually started
When something's not right

Amiable (adj) friendly

To be **amiable** is to be
Nice and pleasant
Giving good cheer
And a smile ever present

Analgesic (n) pain reliever

An **analgesic**
Heals my pain
Allows me to go
Dancing in the rain

<u>Anecdote</u> (n) brief story

An **anecdote**
Is a short aside
A funny story
You can provide

<u>Animated</u> (adj) lively

An **animated** person
Jumps up and down
They can have on
A smile or a frown

<u>Annul</u> (v) to cancel

After agreeing to **annul**
The marriage
Plans were scraped
For the baby carriage

<u>Anomaly</u> (n) oddity

An **anomaly** is something
That's out of sort
Like a short man
On a basketball court

<u>Anonymous</u> (n) unknown

Someone **anonymous**
You don't know
They could be friend
Or could be foe

<u>Antecedent</u> (n) precursor

Antecedent means something
That came before
Like the revolution
Before the war

<u>Anthology</u> (n) compilation

The Beatles' **Anthology**
Is so very long
Precisely because
It contains all their songs

<u>Antipathy</u> (n) hatred

Antipathy is similar
To a very strong dislike
The feeling most have
Towards Hitler's Third Reich

Antiquated (adj) old-fashioned

Antiquated is old
And out of date
Like the 1960's
Roller-skate

Antiseptic (adj) clean, sterile

Antiseptic means very clean
Where no dirt can be seen

Antithesis (n) the opposite

The **antithesis** of to love
Is to hate
The **antithesis** of my foe
Is my mate

Apathetic (adj) indifferent

He didn't even try
He was so **apathetic**
Such a shame
As he was so athletic

Apprehend (v) to catch

Following his duty
To serve and protect
The policeman **apprehended**
The dangerous suspect

Aquatic and Arboreal (adj)

Arboreal refers to leaves and trees
Aquatic refers to water and seas

Arcane (adj) mysterious

Something **arcane**
Is only known by a few
Like a secret code
Or a hidden clue

Archaic (adj) obsolete

Something **archaic**
Is outdated and old
Like a monetary system
Based upon gold

<u>Arid</u> (adj) dry

Arid environments are very dry
Places with little water supply

<u>Artifacts</u> (n) antique

Artifacts come from
Civilizations of old
Like a Mayan statue
Covered with mold

<u>Artisan</u> (n) craftsman

A fine **artisan** is a
Craftsman that has skill
Someone you appreciate
Until you get the bill

<u>Ascertain</u> (v) to determine

To **ascertain**
Is to figure out
Like what this vocab word
Is all about

Ascetic (adj) self-denying

To live **ascetic**
Is to practice self denial
Lent is like
A forty day trial

Ascribe (v) to attribute

To **ascribe** is to give
Credit to others
Whether willingly
Or against your druthers

Aspersion (n) an insulting remark

You cast an **aspersion**
If you attack my reputation
If you do it falsely
It's considered defamation

Aspire (v) to desire

When you **aspire**
You follow your dream
No matter how hard
Getting there may seem

<u>Assail</u> (v) to attack

When you **assail**
You are attacking
Trying your best
To send someone packing

<u>Assess</u> (v) to evaluate

To evaluate
Is to **assess**
So you can make
An educated guess

<u>Assiduous</u> (adj) diligent

The **assiduous** employee
Is a hard working man
Always tries his best
To do whatever he can

<u>Assuage</u> (v) to ease

The storm stopped
The sky began to clear
That did much to
Assuage her fear

Astute (adj) smart

Jan was smart
Astute indeed
Her answers were correct
100% guaranteed

Atone (v) to make amends

To **atone** is to make amends
For something done wrong
Fred finally admitted
He was at fault all along

Atrophy (v) to waste away

Atrophy is not a medal to win
Instead it means to decay
Like your muscles can do
If you don't exercise and play

Attain (v) to achieve

To **attain**
Means to achieve
Reaching goals
In which you believe

Atypical (adj) unusual

Very **atypical**
Which means not normal
Would describe the guy
Who wore shorts to a formal

Audacious (adj) very bold, daring

Something **audacious**
Is excessively bold
Like going to Fort Knox
To steal a pile of gold

Audible (adj) capable of being heard

Something **audible**
Can be heard
Like the sharp cries
Of a baby bird

Auspicious (adj) favorable

A promising beginning
Is an **auspicious** start
Like having great weather
When our sail boats depart

Austere (adj) harsh

Something **austere**
Is bare and bleak
Like a desert environment
It makes one weak

Avarice (n) greed

The king had **avarice**
An enormous greed
Gave all to himself
None to those in need

Aversion (n) a great dislike

Big Bob has
An **aversion** to bees
Once he spots one
He always flees

Balk (v) to resist

Jane asked for a ring
Her boyfriend **balked**
So she picked up her things
And away she walked

Bane (n) something that ruins or spoils

The **bane** of my existence
Is 5th period gym
Afterward I feel pain
In each and every limb

Bard (n) ancient poet

A **bard** is a poet
From the Middle Ages
Their compositions
Fill countless pages

Bashful (adj) timid, shy

The **bashful** girl
Was quite shy
Would never talk
To any cute guy

Beguile (v) to deceive

To **beguile** is to trick or deceive
Like making a prank call
That your neighbors believe

Behemoth (n) something huge

Something that's **behemoth**
Is huge in size and power
It can intimidate many
And cause them to cower

Benevolent (adj) kind

The **benevolent** dictator
Was good and kind
His rule was fair
His justice blind

Benign (adj) not harmful

Thankfully, the tumor was **benign**
No sight of cancer in my spine

Berate (v) to scold

To **berate** is to scold
Scream and yell
As loud as a ringing
Fire alarm bell

Beseech (v) to beg

To **beseech** is to beg
Even to plead
Like the crook wanting
Leniency for his bad deed

Bilk (v) to defraud

Bernie Madoff **bilked**
His clients of money
Now he sits in jail
Where it's not too sunny

Blemish (n) a flaw, stain

A **blemish** is a flaw
Like an acne spot
It often looks like
A big red dot

Blight (n) devastation

Something wrought
With lots of **blight**
Is usually not
A pretty sight

Boisterous (adj) loud, rowdy

Boisterous boys
Are noisy and loud
Just a few can
Sound like a crowd

Bombastic (adj) pompous

The player was **bombastic**
Had an inflated ego
Not someone I would
Like to call my amigo

Brazen (adj) bold

The **brazen** crook
Was shamelessly bold
He stole people's hats
When it was cold

Brusque (adj) impolitely abrupt

Brusque is short, abrupt
And often rough
Like the demeanor of a cop
Who is quick to cuff

Burnish (v) to polish

To **burnish** is to
Polish or shine
Like cleaning a coin
To reveal a sparkling dime

Buttress (v) to give support

To **buttress**
Is to support
Like the columns
At the Supreme Court

Cajole (v) to persuade

Cajole means to coax
And often to urge
Like telling your friend
To buy the Plasma and splurge

Calamity (n) disaster

Named for disaster
There once was a dame
Who went by the moniker
Calamity Jane

Calibrate (v) to adjust

The trusty mechanic
Calibrated the wheels
He fixed the problem
That made them squeal

Callous (adj) insensitive

Sarah was quite **callous**
Her demeanor cold and mean
Though the prettiest girl in school
She'd never win prom queen

Camaraderie (n) friendship

The team had **camaraderie**
They were very close
After the season ended
That's what they missed the most

Candid (adj) honest

Jim was **candid**
He spoke from the heart
Told me my choices
Were not very smart

Capacious (adj) roomy

The new gym was **capacious**
Much bigger than before
Now we can have two games
Playing on the same floor

Capricious (adj) impulsive

The **capricious** boy
Couldn't concentrate at all
With his mind and body
Bouncing off the wall

Captivate (v) to fascinate

The **captivating** movie
Had the audience enthralled
As the somber film ended
The moviegoers bawled

Caroused (v) to party

After arriving at college
Bob **caroused** and partied
Until he got kicked out
For always being tardy

Caucus (n) political conference

In politics, a gathering
Is often called a **caucus**
Some can be serene
Others quite raucous

Cerebral (adj) intellectual

Tom was **cerebral**
He was very smart
With his eye glasses
He even looked the part

Cherish (v) to value greatly

Sam **cherished** his first car
It looked spotless everyday
His girlfriend wished
Sam loved her the same way

Circuitous (adj) indirect, circular

The lawyer's **circuitous** argument
Went around and around
The jury was not convinced
So a guilty verdict was found

Circumvent (v) to go around

At the Renaissance Fair
The man **circumvented** the rule
By bringing a pistol
To a sword only duel

Clairvoyant (adj) psychic

The psychic Miss Cleo
Dressed very flamboyant
She could see into the future
So she was **clairvoyant**

Clamor (n) a persistent loud noise

The boy banged the pans
And made such a **clamor**
That his mom ran out
To see what was the matter

Clandestine (adj) secret

The spy had a secret meeting
It was a **clandestine** affair
He passed the classified envelope
To the man in the black chair

Clergy (n) people of the church

Someone in the **clergy**
Is part of the church
They spend much time
Doing Bible research

Cloying (adj) overly sweet

Cloying remarks are too much
They are excessively sweet
They come off as creepy
Which makes girls retreat

Coalesce (v) to unite

The band's eclectic sound
Coalesces into one song
All the parts fit together
And it ends with a gong

Cobbler (n) shoemaker

A **cobbler** fixes
And repairs shoes
In every color
From red to blue

Cognizant (adj) aware

I was **cognizant**
Which means aware
That in love and war
All is fair

Coherent (adj) clear, understandable

Mike was **coherent**
After the crash
Gave a detailed account
Of the smash

Colloquial (adj) informal

Colloquial is informal conversation
It ain't high level communication

Complacent (n)   satisfied

Sally got **complacent**
She had a good grade
But didn't study hard
And saw her A fade

Compress (v) to press together

To **compress**
Means to apply pressure
After a cut
This is a first aid measure

Concede (v) to admit

The husband **conceded**
That his wife was right
Hoping to end
The nasty fight

Concise (adj) brief, to the point

Something that's **concise**
Is short, succinct
And often precise

Concoct (v) to invent or fabricate

Forgetting his homework
Jon **concocted** a tale
His teacher didn't believe him
And told him 'You're going to fail'

Concord (n) an agreement

Sounding similar
The word **concord**
Is a synonym for
The word accord

Condone (v) to pardon, overlook

The prosecutor refused
To **condone** the company's actions
He did not excuse the many
Illegal transactions

Conduit (n) a channel

A **conduit** is a channel
Through which something passes
Like a car's exhaust pipe
Which gets rid of gasses

Confection (n) sweetened food

A **confection** is
A delicious cake
And other yummy
Things you bake

Conflagration (n) a fire

A **conflagration**
Is a great fire
Its flames shoot
Higher and higher

Consolation (n) something of comfort

I lost the race
Missed the celebration
But got a T-shirt
As a **consolation**

Constituent (n) citizen

To remain in office
The congressman was smart
He followed his **constituents**
Desires from the start

Construe (v) interpret, decipher

While vacationing in England
Becky had to **construe**
What was the meaning
Of the funny word 'Loo'

Consumption (n) the purchase of goods

Consumption is key
When calculating GDP

Contentious (adj) controversial

The **contentious** dispute
Between the men of ill repute
Ended in a lengthy lawsuit

Contusion (n) a bruise

A **contusion**
Is a brusin'

Conundrum (n) difficult problem, puzzle

A **conundrum** is a problem
That's hard to solve
You need patience and
A good deal of resolve

Convene (v) to gather, assemble

To **convene** is to come together
Like birds of a feather

Convoluted (adj) complex

The **convoluted** plot
Made no sense
The entire movie
Lacked suspense

Cosmopolitan (adj) sophisticated

Sophisticated and worldly
Elle was **cosmopolitan**
Had an eclectic taste
And loved Neapolitan

Covert (adj) done in secret

The soldier was engaged
In **covert** action
Against the country's
Rival faction

Curt (adj) short, terse

Steve asked out Lilly
Her reply was **curt**
An abrupt 'No!'
His feelings were hurt

Debacle (n) a disaster, a fiasco

The prom was a **debacle**
Everything went wrong
The DJ didn't even
Play one good song

Debauchery (n) indulgence in pleasures

Spring Break arrived
Debauchery ensued
The students acted
Inappropriate and lewd

Debunk (v) discredit

The scientist was wrong
His hypothesis **debunked**
His colleagues wondered
If Chemistry he flunked

Deface (v) to damage

Our mascot was **defaced**
It was damaged and marred
The school decided
To hire a guard

Deft (adj) skillful

The **deft** skier
Never missed a gate
He counts his medals
In multiples of eight

Defunct (adj) no longer in existence

Something **defunct** is no more
That boarded up building
Was once a store

Deliberate (v) to consider carefully

The jury **deliberates**
They think things through
They look over the evidence
And piece together the clues

Demure (adj) quiet, shy

Someone **demure**
Is calm and quiet
Quite the opposite
Of Jen who's a riot

<u>Denounce</u> (v) criticize

After the dead fish was found
The Principal announced
The pranksters were in trouble
Their actions **denounced**

<u>Derelict</u> (adj) abandoned

The **derelict** neighborhood
Was in extremely bad shape
Couldn't even be fixed
By a superhero in a cape

<u>Desolate</u> (adj) barren, deserted

Desolate and deserted
Was the abandoned school
The hallways were empty
And so was the pool

<u>Destitute</u> (adj) poor

Destitute people are poor
And in need
They are whom
Soup kitchens feed

Devious (adj) tricky, deceitful

The **devious** clerk
Was deceitful and tricky
Stole merchandise
Then gave it to Nicky

Diligent (adj) hard-working

The **diligent** boy
Tried everyday
To study hard
And raise his grade

Diminutive (adj) very small

The **diminutive** poodle
Is very small
About the size
Of a toy doll

Dirge (n) funeral song

Played at the funeral
The **dirge** was sad
Tough for the kids
To bury their dad

Disaffected (adj) rebellious

The teens rebelled
Like **disaffected** youth
They lacked refinement
And were labeled uncouth

Disavow (v) to deny any knowledge of

The Professor **disavowed**
Any knowledge
Of the overnight break-in
At the college

Discern (v) to determine

Robert **discerned**
And then detected
If he asked Amy out
He would be rejected

Disclose (v) to reveal

To **disclose** is to reveal
The opposite of conceal

Discursive (adj) rambling

Mr. Smith liked to ramble
His lectures were so **discursive**
That I resorted to doodling
On the desk in cursive

Disgruntled (adj) dissatisfied

The **disgruntled** accountant
Was quite upset
That his client failed
To pay his debt

Dispatch (v) to send

Reinforcements were **dispatched**
They were sent to the battlefield
Hoping to win the fight
So victory could be sealed

Dispel (v) eliminate

The doctor **dispelled** the rumor
That the lump was a tumor

Disperse (v) to scatter

The house party was rocking
But it quickly **dispersed**
The parents came home
The kids feared the worst

Dissipate (v) to disappear

The rain **dissipated**
The sun shone through
The clouds parted
The sky was blue

Dissonance (n) conflict

Cognitive **dissonance**
Is a psychology term
Meaning you have two beliefs
That do not affirm

Dissuade (v) discourage

Mike **dissuaded** Ben
From cheating on the test
He told him to study hard
And try his very best

Dither (v) to hesitate

To **dither** is to dawdle
And to delay
Lazy people do this
Every single day

Divisive (adj) disruptive

Angie's actions were **divisive**
She broke up Emma and Jim
Because every single day
She called and texted him

Divulge (v) to disclose

The suspect relented
And **divulged** the information
Which helped the police
With their investigation

Docile (adj) easy to train, obedient

The puppy was **docile**
It was easily trained
It soon didn't need
To ever be chained

<u>Dour</u> (adj) unfriendly

The gloomy town
Looked very **dour**
Until we planted
Radiant flowers

<u>Eclectic</u> (adj) diverse

The **eclectic** band
Plays many styles
Causing their fans
Many smiles

<u>Ecstatic</u> (adj) very happy

Not wanting to shift
Hillary was **ecstatic**
That her new car
Was an automatic

<u>Edict</u> (n) law

A brand new **edict**
Was issued by the King
That said all subjects
Must search with Bing

<u>Effervescent</u> (adj) lively, bubbly

Lynn was lively and
Effervescent
She was bright like a
Fluorescent

<u>Egregious</u> (adj) very bad

The student's actions
Were **egregious**
His bad behavior
Less than prestigious

<u>Elated</u> (adj) excited

Jack was **elated**
School was done
He graduated
His new life begun

<u>Eloquent</u> (adj) articulate

His essay was **eloquent**
Forceful and expressive
Many college admissions
Thought it was impressive

Elude (v) to avoid, evade

To **elude** is to evade
By yourself or with an aide

Embezzle (v) commit fraud

The accountant **embezzled**
He stole the money
The CEO noticed
The numbers looked funny

Encumber (v) burden

To burden or weigh down
Is to **encumber**
Like when you're carrying
A pile of lumber

Enigmatic (adj) mysterious

The mysterious man
Is **enigmatic**
Every day he hides
In the attic

Ephemeral (adj) short lived

Ephemeral is short-lived
Or fleeting
Like our chance
Airport meeting

Epistolary (adj)   writing letters

The relationship was **epistolary**
We wrote many a letter
This communication style
Made my writing better

Epitome (n) the ideal

Pat was the **epitome**
Of a good friend
He was always there
With a hand to lend

Erudite (adj) scholarly

The **erudite** Professor
Has great knowledge
For 27 years
He's been teaching college

Esoteric (adj) understood by only a few

The **esoteric** theory
Was hard to understand
It didn't help matters
That the course was so bland

Exacerbate (v) to make worse

Exacerbate is to
Make worse
Like losing your keys
And then your purse

Exalt (v) to praise

When you **exalt**
You give praise
Like we do to LeBron
For his dunks that amaze

Excavate (v) to unearth, dig out

The archeologist
Excavated the fossil
He dug up a dinosaur
That was truly colossal

Exhort (v) to urge

The soccer coach
Exhorted the team
To put in more effort
And pick up steam

Exorbitant (adj) very high

Went to Vegas
Paid an **exorbitant** price
For one bad roll
Of the risky dice

Expunge (v) to erase

After two years
Dave's record will be
Expunged of
His stealing spree

Fabricate (v) to make up

To **fabricate** is to make up
Like an excuse you dream up

Fastidious (adj) demanding, picky

To be **fastidious**
Is to be hard to please
You are picky, choosy
And never at ease

Fathom (v) to understand

I cannot **fathom**
Nor understand
Why a new moon mission
Is not planned

Fervent (adj) passionate

The **fervent** fan
Loved the team
If they won
He would beam

<u>Fickle</u> (adj) inconsistent

The **fickle** fan
Backed only the winner
Changed his allegiance
By the time it was dinner

<u>Flabbergasted</u> (adj) stunned

Flabbergasted is a big word
Definitely oversized
But it simply means to be
Astounded and surprised

<u>Flagrant</u> (adj) exceptionally bad

The **flagrant** foul
Was wrong and egregious
Far from honorable
Or prestigious

<u>Flouting</u> (v) deliberately disobeying

Flouting the dress code
Justin did not care
That he walked the halls
In his underwear

Forage (v) to search for food

On the camping trip
They **foraged** for food
Couldn't find any
It dampened their mood

Forestall (v) to prevent

To **forestall** an attack
Is to try and delay
Attempting to keep
Your enemies at bay

Fraught (adj) filled

Hitchhiking is **fraught**
With danger
Putting yourself at the mercy
Of a stranger

Frenetic (adj) frantic, chaotic

The **frenetic** pace of the game
Was so fast
Jim didn't realize how much time
Had passed

<u>Frivolous</u> (adj) not worthy of merit, trivial

Frivolous lawsuits
Are not worthy of the court
Many are filed
Under the law of tort

<u>Frugal</u> (adj) thrifty

The old man was **frugal**
He was very thrifty
Never spent more
Than two dollars fifty

<u>Garish</u> (adj) brash, gaudy

The jacket was **garish**
Gaudy and bold
The sleeves were completely
Covered in gold

<u>Genial</u> (adj) pleasant

To be **genial** means
To be pleasant and kind
A person like the Dalai Lama
Comes quickly to mind

Gluttony (n) excessive eating & drinking

Gluttony is eating too much
To overindulge and binge
That's why it's one of
The seven deadly sins

Goad (v) to prompt (by irritation)

Tina **goaded** Kate into a fight
She called her names
Then threw a left and a right

Grandiose (adj) extravagant

Peter had a **grandiose** dream
Of being crowned king
And having the chance to wear
All that fancy bling

Hallowed (adj) sacred

Arlington National Cemetery
Is considered **hallowed** ground
Reverence is expected
People hardly make a sound

Hapless (adj) unlucky

The **hapless** team was
Both bad and unlucky
Lost every game
Including Kentucky

Harrowing (adj) traumatic

At the theme park
It was a **harrowing** ride
The rollercoaster shook us
From side to side

Hegemonic (adj) dominating influence

There are those that say
That the U.S. of A's
Hegemonic power
Is fading away

Heinous (adj) despicable, terrible

A **heinous** crime
Is particularly cruel
It will certainly get you
Expelled from school

<u>Hiatus</u> (n) break

A **hiatus** is a break
Or a reprieve
Like your school takes
Over New Year's Eve

<u>Ignominious</u> (adj) humiliating

Ignominious is to be in disgrace
A humiliating experience one might face

<u>Illicit</u> (adj) banned

There is a list of **illicit** things
That are not allowed in school
To bring any of them to class
Would be breaking the rule

<u>Immerse</u> (v) to be deeply involved

Joe **immersed** himself
In his studies
Never went out to play
With his buddies

Immutable (adj) unchanging

The laws of physics
Are considered **immutable**
They cannot be changed
And are indisputable

Impassive (adj) unemotional

The **impassive** policeman
Didn't even cry
When he saw the aftermath
Of the violent drive-by

Impecunious (adj) poor

To be **impecunious**
Is to be very poor
It can be a major obstacle
And close many doors

Imperious (adj) domineering

The **imperious** teacher
Was quite domineering
Her bossy demeanor
Was opposite of endearing

Impervious (adj) impenetrable

The warm fleece gloves
Were **impervious** to arctic air
They blocked out the cold
You should definitely get a pair!

Impetuous (adj) impulsive

An **impetuous** decision
Is one that is rash
No thought is put in
It's done in a flash

Implacable (adj) inflexible

The teacher was **implacable**
She couldn't be appeased
I studied so hard
And received only D's

Implicate (v) incriminate

After he was caught
Paul **implicated** Dan
Said he was the one
Who came up with the plan

Inane (adj) pointless

Steve always asked
Questions that were **inane**
They were meaningless
With no value to gain

Incessant (adj) nonstop

The **incessant** sirens
Would never end
Living next to a fire house
I would not recommend

Incisive (adj) insightful

Clear, sharp and direct
Her rebuttal was **incisive**
To the outcome of the case
It was most decisive

Inclination (n) tendency

Jim is not even aware
Of his **inclination** to swear

Incorrigible (adj) uncontrollable

The **incorrigible** kid
Could not be controlled
He ran around and
Never did as he was told

Indolent (adj) lazy

Having no work ethic
The kids are **indolent** and lazy
Instead of studying for school
They would rather pick daisies

Indomitable (adj) invincible

The Spanish Armada
Was an **indomitable** fleet
It seemed as if
They could never be beat

Inexorable (adj) unchanging

The teacher was **inexorable**
She couldn't be persuaded
To make today's quiz
Completely ungraded

Inimical (adj) unfriendly, cold

An **inimical** advisor
Mr. Paul would resist
To offer any help
And would never assist

Innocuous (adj) harmless

Something **innocuous**
Does no harm
Like seeing a rabbit
Is no cause for alarm

Insolent (adj) rude

Being **insolent** is
Like being rude
You are arrogant
And have a bad attitude

Interminable (adj) never-ending

Interminable lectures
Keep going and going
With no end in sight
Or even slowing

Intransigent (adj) inflexible

The **intransigent** man
Refused to compromise
He didn't want to debate
Instead he resorted to lies

Intrepid (adj) fearless

The **intrepid** explorer
Conquered the mountain K2
He braved the conditions
As the strong winds blew

Irascible (adj) easily angered

The bully was **irascible**
He was hot-headed
Seeing him in the hallways
Was something I dreaded

Laconic (adj) using very few words

Laconic is a writing style
That is short and terse
Forgoing wordiness
Like this rhyming verse

Languish (v) to lose strength or energy

During the Bar exam
You fade and **languish**
Its difficulty and length
Creates much mental anguish

Largess (n) generosity

My boss showed **largess**
When he gave an expensive gift
It was a generous reward
For excelling on my shift

Lenient (adj) easygoing

The teacher was **lenient**
And showed much restraint
By accepting my paper
That was two weeks late

Lithe (adj) flexible

The ice skater's body
Was flexible and **lithe**
Her routine was fun
Happy and blithe

<u>Lucid</u> (adj) easy to understand, clear

The witness was **lucid**
Easy to understand
He spoke very clearly
When he took the stand

<u>Luminous</u> (adj) glowing

The diamond was **luminous**
It shined so bright
Much to my girlfriend's
Giddy delight

<u>Lurid</u> (adj) shocking

Tabloids frequently publish
Lurid and sensational tales
Hoping you buy them
To read the dirty details

<u>Magnanimous</u> (adj) generous, noble

To be **magnanimous**
Is to be generous and noble
Like those who start charities
To help causes that are global

Malevolent (adj) mean, malicious

If you are **malevolent**
You want to cause harm
Like setting a fire
And disabling the alarm

Mandate (n) an order

A **mandate** is an
Authoritative command
That you must follow
And understand

Maudlin (adj) sappy, sentimental

The movie was **maudlin**
Sentimental and sappy
I had to watch it
To make my wife happy

Medley (n) assortment

A **medley** consists
Of a variety of things
A musical one has
Many songs to sing

Mercurial (adj) changeable, erratic

James was **mercurial**
His attitude changed all the time
One minute angry
The next feeling sublime

Meritorious (adj) worthy of praise

The fallen soldier was
Considered **meritorious**
For his actions that were
Honorable and glorious

Meticulous (adj) thorough, careful

Brittney was careful with details
Her bookkeeping was **meticulous**
Wanda thought it was obsessive
And somewhat ridiculous

Mitigate (v) to lessen

The doctor injected medicine
To **mitigate** and lessen the pain
It was administered through IV
Which means it went in the vein

<u>Modicum</u> (n) a small amount

A **modicum** is a small amount
Hardly much of any to count

<u>Mollify</u> (v) to make calmer

The police tried to calm the crowd
And **mollify** the situation
Lessen the people's anger
And decrease the frustration

<u>Mores</u> (n) customs, moral values

Mores are the moral values
Of a distinct group
Originating from family
Country or Boy Scout troop

<u>Morose</u> (adj) depressed, glum

Jackie was always **morose**
Acting gloomy and glum
Meet her when you're happy
And your high she would bum

Nadir (n) the lowest point

My first day of boot camp
Was already a disaster
But the **nadir** came
When I met my drill master

Nascent (adj) starting to develop

Estonia and Latvia
Are **nascent** nations
They are slowly building
Sustainable foundations

Nefarious (adj)   wicked, evil

The villain's **nefarious** plan
Was wicked and cruel
He would stop at nothing
Until the world he would rule

Nomadic (adj) wandering

Nomadic people move
From place to place
They inhabit no
Designated space

Noxious (adj) harmful, dangerous

During chemistry
We wore glasses
To protect our eyes
From **noxious** gases

Nuance (n) a subtle difference

Nuance means a subtle variation
Like knowing the difference
Between a country and a nation

Obfuscate (v) to confuse

The politician **obfuscated** the facts
Which means he made them unclear
He did this on purpose
To make the scandal disappear

Obsolete (adj) outdated

Super Nintendo was once
Hard to beat
But now with the Xbox 360
It's considered **obsolete**

Vocabulary | Rhyminders

<u>Obstinate</u> (adj) stubborn

The **obstinate** child was stubborn
He didn't follow the rules
He wanted things his way
And got kicked out of many schools

<u>Odious</u> (adj) horrible

Cleaning the septic tank
Was an **odious** task
Bob hated the job
The smells he couldn't mask

<u>Ominous</u> (adj) threatening

The **ominous** clouds
Provided a warning
Their dark color meant
It would soon be storming

<u>Onerous</u> (adj) unpleasant, burdensome

Homework can be **onerous**
Very time-consuming
Every night I come home
There's a big pile looming

Opulent (adj) lavish, luxurious

The lavish and **opulent** home
Belonged to the rock stars
It had three fountains
And a garage for many cars

Ostentatious (adj) showy, pretentious

The gold bricked driveway
Was considered **ostentatious**
It was intended to impress
But looked showy and tasteless

Ostracized (v) to exclude, shun

If you are **ostracized**
You are excluded
You are not accepted
And live secluded

Palliate (v) to make less severe

The nurse worked to
Palliate the patient's pain
She relieved their discomfort
While treating the sprain

Pallid (adj) colorless

The **pallid** sky
Was very gray
Void of color
Day after day

Panacea (n) a cure for everything

A **panacea** is a cure
For all that ills
Doctors wish they could find
These magic pills

Paragon (n) the model or ideal

Liz was considered
The **paragon** student
She got all A's
And was very prudent

Pariah (n) a social outcast

An outcast was Mariah
She was rejected from society
And considered a **pariah**

<u>Partisan</u> (n) a strong supporter

Partisan politics
Is a term you hear
Politicians side with their party
Never giving others an ear

<u>Pejorative</u> (adj) derogatory

Suzy replied with a
Pejorative remark
A negative comment
That's mean like a bark

<u>Penchant</u> (n) a strong liking for

Chelsea always had
A **penchant** for steak
Being a chef, her penchant
Was easy to make

<u>Penultimate</u> (adj) second to last

If you were **penultimate**
It means you were next to last
If you were in a race
You wouldn't be very fast

Perfunctory (adj) showing little interest

The **perfunctory** attitude
Was not well received
The jury felt the murderer
Should have been more bereaved

Perusal (n) a careful examination

Perusal is a look over or review
Like studying a puzzle for a clue

Pervasive (adj) spread everywhere

The water flowed
The flood was **pervasive**
It spread all over
To far off places

Petulant (adj) bad-tempered

The boy's **petulant** behavior
Was grouchy and rude
He was always involved
In some sort of feud

Philanthropic (adj) charitable

The **philanthropic** comedian
Gave all his money
To causes he believed in
Both serious and funny

Pillage (v) to forcefully seize in war

The army **pillaged** and plundered
They stole all our stuff
It's as if the war
Was not tough enough

Pittance (n) small amount

A **pittance** is a
Very small amount
Usually money is what
They are talking about

Placate (v) appease

To **placate**
Is to appease
Like smiling when
Your grandma says 'Cheese!'

<u>Placid</u> (adj) calm

The **placid** lake
Was very calm
We relaxed by
The Royal Palms

<u>Platitude</u> (n) unoriginal

A **platitude** is like a cliché
Something uninspired to say

<u>Plethora</u> (n) too many, overabundance

Nat has a **plethora**
Of designer shoes
She has a dozen pair
Of Jimmy Choos

<u>Pliable</u> (adj) flexible

The gymnast was **pliable**
Her body could contort
Into various shapes
To excel at her sport

<u>Poignant</u> (adj) emotional, touching

The **poignant** film
Was very affecting
Much more emotional
Than I was expecting

<u>Pragmatic</u> (adj) practical

To be practical
Is to be **pragmatic**
Like keeping your distance
From a crazed fanatic

<u>Precocious</u> (adj) intelligent, gifted

The **precocious** child
Is ahead of her peers
She has been learning calculus
For more than two years

<u>Presumptuous</u> (adj) overconfident

The coach was **presumptuous**
Thought he would win
Decided to wait to
Put his starters in

Pretense (n) pretending

Unbeknownst to her parents
Brooke went out on a date
Under the **pretense**
She went out just to skate

Proclivity (n) a tendency

Mike had a **proclivity**
Toward racing cars
His appetite for speed
Landed him behind bars

Procure (v) obtain, acquire

The terrorists wanted to **procure**
Which means acquire
Many dangerous weapons
That they desire

Profuse (adj) plentiful

Something **profuse**
Is abundantly found
Like blades of grass
Which cover the ground

Propensity (n) a preference, tendency

Some women have
A **propensity** to consume
Large amounts
Of luxury perfume

Prosaic (adj) dull

Prosaic is boring
It leads to snoring

Proscribe (v) ban, make illegal

When you **proscribe** you outlaw
Like dry counties and alcohol

Prowess (n) superior ability

The student's musical **prowess**
Could not be ignored
She had an amazing ability
To hit the right chords

Prudent (adj) careful, sensible

The **prudent** investor
Avoided financial dangers
Never trusted advice
From shady strangers

Pugnacious (adj) aggressive

Adam was **pugnacious**
Always getting into fights
It seemed he had a quarrel
Every single night

Pungent (adj) a strong taste or smell

The **pungent** odor
Was quite strong
We had to smell it
All day long

Quaint (adj) old-fashioned, charming

The **quaint** village
Was different than our own
Being old fashioned
It didn't have a phone

Quandary (n) dilemma

Becca was in **quandary**
She was in a dilemma
Should she invite James
And disinvite Emma?

Quell (v) to suppress

The violence was **quelled**
It was suppressed
The General said
The mission was a success

Rapport (n) bond, relationship

Mike and Jeff
Had a good **rapport**
Became instant friends
After joining the Marine Corps

Rash (adj) sudden, reckless

A **rash** decision
Is one that's made quick
Like breaking-up by email
With only a click

Raucous (adj) loud and disorderly

The **raucous** crowd
Was lively and loud

Raze (v) to tear down, demolish

Raze does not mean go higher
It means to demolish or flatten
Like old buildings are done
For new ones in Manhattan

Rebuke (v) to criticize sharply

Rebuke is to
Criticize or scold
Rebuking a President
Is certainly bold

Reciprocate (v) to give in return, respond

When you **reciprocate**
You give something back
He gave you a punch
So you give him a whack

Reclusive (adj) withdrawn, secluded

The **reclusive** author
Was always alone
He didn't give interviews
In person or by phone

Refute (v) to disprove

The accused man **refuted**
The claims he was at fault
He presented evidence
That cleared him of assault

Relish (v) to enjoy

Not just a condiment
To **relish** means to enjoy
Like you do when you play
With your brand new toy

Remedial (adj) designed to improve

When I got to college
I had to take **remedial** classes
It turned out my knowledge
Was well below the masses

Vocabulary | Rhyminders

<u>Remiss</u> (v) negligent

I would be **remiss**
Which means neglectful
If I didn't tell you
How you were so helpful

<u>Renowned</u> (n) famous

The **renowned** astronaut
Was honored and acclaimed
He even had babies
For which he was named

<u>Repentant</u> (adj) regretful

The **repentant** driver
Apologized again
Said he never intended
To hurt those men

<u>Replete</u> (adj) full

The buffet was **replete**
With many kinds of cheese
My stomach was saying
'Feed me, please!'

<u>Repose</u> (v) rest

After a long day of work
I wanted to **repose**
As I laid down
I soon began to doze

<u>Reprehensible</u> (adj) deserving of blame

Cheating on the test
Is **reprehensible** and wrong
Nowhere in school
Does this behavior belong

<u>Reprieve</u> (n) a temporary delay

The teacher granted a **reprieve**
A temporary delay
Until the student could find
The missing essay

<u>Repudiate</u> (v) to reject

Matt **repudiated** her claims
Which means he rejected
The false accusations
That he was connected

<u>Rescind</u> (v) to take back

Tim **rescinded** the offer
He took it back
He no longer wanted
The Honda in black

<u>Resilient</u> (adj) tough

The **resilient** horse
Never backed down
It withstood adversity
And won the Triple Crown

<u>Respite</u> (n) a period of rest

A **respite** is when you take
A brief relaxing break

<u>Resplendent</u> (adj) shining, radiant

The **resplendent** dress
Stood out from the others
Because of its shiny
Bright, beautiful colors

<u>Retract</u> (v) to take back, withdraw

The statement was **retracted**
It was withdrawn
You could no longer find it
Because it was gone

<u>Revel</u> (v) to party

The partiers **revel**
Into the night
They had much fun
Were quick to excite

<u>Revoke</u> (v) to take away, cancel

After getting 5 tickets
Lisa's license was **revoked**
She could no longer drive
Her freedom was choked

<u>Rife</u> (adj) full of

The essay was **rife** with errors
The teacher gave her a D
The student didn't use spell check
Otherwise she'd have a B

Ruminate (v) to ponder

When you **ruminate**
You contemplate

Sagacity (n) wisdom

If you have **sagacity**
You make judgments that are good
You have a great perspective
And have things understood

Sanguine (adj) optimistic

If you are **sanguine**
You are optimistic and cheerful
Just the opposite
Of someone who's fearful

Satiate (v) to fill to excess

Kevin was **satiated**
After the buffet
He ate so much
He didn't eat for a day

Scathing (adj) harsh criticism

The **scathing** report was
Harsh and critical
The Senator thought
It was all political

Serendipity (n) good luck

Lauren had **serendipity**
And good luck
When she discovered
Her stolen truck

Serene (adj) peaceful, calm

Calm and **serene**
Was the island resort
We only disliked
That our stay was so short

Solicitous (adj) attentive

While in the hospital
Sam got **solicitous** attention
With all the nice nurses
He opted for a 2 day extension

Vocabulary | Rhyminders

Soluble (adj) able to be disolved

Soluble dissolves in water
An example is Vitamin B
Non-soluble does not
Which is the case of Vitamin D

Somnolent (adj) sleepy

The **somnolent** child
Fell asleep in class
He was always sleepy
Did the same during Mass

Sophomoric (adj) immature

The **sophomoric** prank
Was quite immature
The principal said
Suspensions are assured

Sovereign (adj) self-rule, autonomous

A basic tenet of
Sovereign rights
Is to defend your country
With all your might

Stagnate (v) to lack development

Steve's skills **stagnated**
They didn't improve
He stopped practicing
Never reclaimed his groove

Staid (adj) reserved, formal

The **staid** man
Was always sedate
Never loosened his collar
Even on a hot date

Stingy (adj) cheap

The **stingy** woman
Was not generous or kind
She always had
Her bank account in mind

Stoic (adj) no reaction

The **stoic** man
Was unaffected by emotion
Didn't even smile
When offered a promotion

<u>Strenuous</u> (adj) demanding, exhausting

The game of basketball
Is a **strenuous** sport
Constantly running
Up and down the court

<u>Subjugate</u> (v) to force into submission

The new rulers of the land
Subjugated the peasants
They forced them to hunt
And cook them pheasants

<u>Succinct</u> (adj) brief and concise

Succinct is concise
And also precise

<u>Superfluous</u> (adj) extra, surplus

It was **superfluous**
To have 3 birthday cakes
I would have been fine
With 1 small cupcake

Surmise (v) to guess

To **surmise** is to infer
Without knowing for sure

Surreptitious (adj) secret, stealthy

The stealthy and
Surreptitious spies
Were covert and
Hidden from our eyes

Surrogate (n) substitute

After the teacher
Had to take leave
A **surrogate** stepped in
To help relieve

Tacit (adj) unspoken, implied

A **tacit** agreement
Is expressed without words
A nod of the head
Is what Charlie preferred

Taciturn (adj) silent

If you are **taciturn**
You do not talk
Instead of speaking
You'd rather walk

Tangential (adj) divergent

The man's response
Was **tangential**
It was irrelevant
And non-essential

Tedious (adj) long and boring

Tedious note taking
Is dull and boring
It's hard to stay focused
And keep from snoring

Temperance (n) moderation

A **temperance** movement
Is against alcohol
The word can also mean
Moderation for all

<u>Tenable</u> (adj) supportable

The wise lawyer offered
Tenable advice
His expertise also
Came with a price

<u>Tenuous</u> (adj) flimsy, weak

A **tenuous** argument
Is rather weak
It won't hold up
In court next week

<u>Tirade</u> (n) an angry speech

After the disappointing loss
The coach went on a **tirade**
He screamed and yelled
About how poor the team played

<u>Tome</u> (n) a large thick book

My backpack contains
War and Peace which is a **tome**
A large and heavy book
That is a pain to carry home

Transgression (n) wrongdoing

A **transgression** is usually
Doing something wrong
Like sneaking in somewhere
You do not belong

Transient (adj) short-term

Tourist towns have a
Transient population
People come and go
For their short vacation

Trepidation (n) fear, anxiety

About to jump out of the plane
Jose felt much **trepidation**
His first time skydiving
Was a scary situation

Trite (adj) stale, commonplace

Unoriginal and common
The comedian's jokes were **trite**
The bored audience laughed
Just to be polite

Truncate (v) to make shorter

The essay was too long
The teacher complained
If you **truncated** the end
Your grade would have gained

Turpitude (n) evil

An act that is **turpitude**
Is immoral and lewd

Ubiquitous (adj) everywhere

Something **ubiquitous**
Is everywhere
On the ground
And in the air

Umbrage (n) offense

I took **umbrage** with that insult
Which means I took offense
The accusations were cruel
I quickly became incensed

<u>Undulate</u> (v) rise and fall, like waves

The water's waves
Undulated at sea
They rippled and rolled
As far as the eye could see

<u>Upbraid</u> (v) to reprimand, scold

Missing curfew again
Megan was **upbraided**
She was scolded severely
And left feeling degraded

<u>Usurp</u> (v) to take by force

The army **usurped**
All the King's power
By raiding the castle
And seizing the tower

<u>Utopia</u> (n) an imagined ideal place

Utopia is a perfect place
That hasn't been found
By the human race

<u>Vacuous</u> (adj) empty, lacking content

The lecture today was **vacuous**
There was no real point
Classes like these
Tend to disappoint

<u>Variegated</u> (adj) variety of colors

The **variegated** box of crayons
Had hundreds of colors and hues
But my absolute favorite
Was the light sky blue

<u>Vehemently</u> (adv) extremely forceful

Steve **vehemently** denied
The accusation
He intensely offered
Another explanation

<u>Venerable</u> (adj) deserving honor

The **venerable** Senator
Has been in office for 20 years
When he was reelected
The crowd broke into cheers

Veracity (n) accuracy, truth

The newspaper editor
Demanded **veracity**
He wanted every word accurate
And checked with tenacity

Verbose (adj) wordy, long-winded

The **verbose** coach told
Longwinded stories
About his past
Pop Warner glories

Vex (v) to puzzle, irritate

Calculus is so **vexing**
Some of the formulas
Are quite perplexing

Vicarious (adj) experience through another

Vicarious means to experience
Through another
Like taking part in sports
By watching your brother

<u>Vigilant</u> (adj) watchful

A Peeping Tom was on the prowl
The town became alert
They were extra **vigilant**
To catch the pervert

<u>Vilify</u> (v) to speak ill of, denounce

The editorial **vilified**
The corrupt politician
It defamed his character
And demanded contrition

<u>Viscous</u> (adj) thick, gluey

Something that's **viscous**
Is sticky and thick
Just like motor oil
Measured with a dipstick

<u>Vivacious</u> (adj) energetic, lively

The **vivacious** woman
Captured all the attention
Her lively demeanor
Was all anyone would mention

<u>Vocation</u> (n) career

I should have chosen
A better **vocation**
This job allows only
Three days vacation

<u>Wily</u> (adj) shrewd, sly

One who is **wily**
Is clever and sly
Like jewel thieves who disappear
In the blink of an eye

<u>Winsome</u> (adj) endearing, charming

Brian's behavior was **winsome**
Charming and appealing
After you meet him
You're left with a good feeling

<u>Wrath</u> (n) anger

Don't be late to class
Or you'll incur her **wrath**
The teacher will be so mad
She'll kick you out of math

Zealot (n) fanatic

A **zealot** is a staunch believer
Their opinions very strong
Those that disagree
Are quite simply wrong

Zenith (n) the highest point

The **zenith** of his career
Was winning the Super Bowl
Nothing would ever top
Kicking that field goal

Zephyr (n) a soft breeze

A **zephyr** is a gentle breeze
That slightly ruffles the leaves